S The $ecret$
C $olors$
G of od

POEMS BY
NANCY THOMAS

THE SECRET COLORS OF GOD
poems by Nancy Thomas

© 2005 by Nancy Thomas

Published by
Barclay Press
Newberg, OR 97132
www.barclaypress.com

Credits can be found on page 127.

Cover design by Donavon L. Aylard
ISBN 1-59498-003-9
Printed in the United States of America

To my family:

David and Debby,
Breanna, Aren, Gwen, Alandra

Jonathan and Kristin,
Reilly, and those yet to be born

Hal.

Muchas gracias.

Many graces.

Contents

The Lights in Your Voice

Both of Us Have Never Been Nuns

Entering the Forest

From Bolivian Mud

A Psalm for High Places

Preface

Behind every poem, a story hides. I've thought it would be fun to include an appendix to this volume and tell all the stories that led to the poems. But that would triple the size of the book and my publisher (who kindly pays the bills) would frown.

So I'll settle for one story, here at the beginning.

I entitled the second section of this book, "Both of Us Have Never Been Nuns," a line from one of the poems. At one point I considered making that line the title of the whole book.

Reactions to this phrase as a title have been interesting. Beginning with a simple puzzled, "What?" people have asked me, "Will Quakers read this?" "Will Catholics be offended?" "What does this have to do with your poetry?" "Does it mean something?" And my favorite, "It sounds just like you!" Hal simply smiled and said, "I like it."

Here's the story behind the poem. For several years I attended a biweekly poetry critique group in Pasadena, California. It was a stimulating experience that not only helped me grow as a poet but gave me friendships that are ongoing.

This was not a Christian group and to some of my fellow poets, the facts that I had served as a missionary in Bolivia and was currently attending seminary were oddities, at best.

One day Mike, the informal leader of the group, asked me in passing, "Nancy, aren't you the one who used to be a nun?" Obviously, nun and missionary flowed together in his mind, both outside the current of his own experience. I just chuckled and set the record straight, but later at home I began thinking of the things I wished I had said. This is not unusual for me, and occasionally a poem will grow out of a real conversation (the "true" part of the poem) that I complete in my imagination (the part I make up that is also true). The fruit of this brief encounter is the poem entitled, "Conversation with Mike on Religion."

I chose a line from the poem, "both of us have never been nuns," as a section title because I like it, too. Every time I read it, I smile. That's a good reason.

But let me back up and make some connections. For me poetry relates to grace, and one of the major roles of a poet is to see and express grace, especially the grace of the ordinary. American poet Robinson Jeffers wrote that "to feel greatly and speak the astonishing beauty of things...is the sole business of poetry." And the "things" Jeffers wrote about were earth, stone, sky, the sea, his dog—the ordinary things of life, where grace ("astonishing beauty") often hides. The secret colors of God.

On my good days, I find grace in any number of places: a memory of my father playing Santa Claus, a lecture on Thomas Jefferson, the agony of a writing deadline, a noisy church service, being stuck in a river, losing a sock in the laundry, real and imaginary conversations and, of course, the relationships they represent. On bad days, I don't find grace anywhere, but that usually means I'm not paying attention.

I find grace in language itself. In words. I love to play with words. It's one of the most serious things I do. The misuse and abuse of words make me angry, and I respond by playing rough. I love slips of the tongue—mine and others'. They usually reflect slips of the brain, occasionally slips of the heart, and the remedy is often a poem.

I love the biblical accounts that link creation, word, and play. God creates the heavens and the earth by the word (Genesis 1). Jesus is alongside as the Logos—the verb of God (John 1). And Wisdom accompanies the Father in the creation romp, "at play in the fields of the Lord" (Proverbs 8). The apostle Paul writes that we, the church, are God's Poem (a very literal translation of Ephesians 2:10), created by the Father for the specific good works we are to do.

As a lover of words, I've been blessed by a life that requires me to know and use several languages other than English (my favorite). The Spanish words related to grace give insight into the poetic role. "Gracia" means pretty much the same in Spanish as it does in English—mercy, undeserved favor, approval, chocolate. What interests me are the related words. "Gracias," as anyone knows, is "thank you" in Spanish, and if you say "muchas gracias" or "mil gracias," you really mean it! Literally, the words mean "graces," "many graces" or, extravagantly, "a thousand graces."

"Gracioso" is another related Spanish grace word, and the common translation is "funny." It's an adjective that goes with clowns, jokes, or small children at play, something that makes you laugh. But literally, it means "full of grace."

So there you have it—links between poetry, grace, play, gratitude, and humor, all grounded in the "humus," the earth of the ordinary. If it seems like I'm starting to go around in circles, you've got it right. But before I begin to explain how circles are more grace-filled than straight lines or sharp angles, I think I'd better stop.

After all, both of us have never been nuns.

Nancy Thomas
Santa Cruz, Bolivia
April 2004

The Lights
in Your
Voice

Third Grade

Rows faced forward military style,
but spring poured in through a wall of windows.
Jellyfish and sea anemones
waved between strands of fixed kelp on the bulletin board.
Above the blackboard the cursive letters of the alphabet
swam in a race to the door.
Mrs. King taught us gull droppings, barnacles,
and the moon's strange dance with the sea.
She also taught us the mystery and music of words.
I titled my first poem, "Tide Pool Life," and began it,
"Oh, how I love to go down to the shore,"
but somewhere in the middle the poem grabbed me,
an undertow I couldn't resist.
There in the second seat, third row, I learned
how language splays like starfish, stings like salt.
Through scratches on paper I began to breathe underwater,
dive for the treasure on the bottom.
Mrs. King—did she know what she was doing?—pushed me
beyond tide pools.
Ever since bits of seaweed cling to my hair.
Words swim like minnows through my brain.
All the windows are open.   ❀

The Contest

When the bell sounded
the end of recess
we would fill our mouths
with water from the drinking fountain,
then file in to our desks.
The contest was to see who could hold
the water longest without swallowing,
choking, or getting called on
to answer some dumb question.
I usually managed for an hour
at a time. The water grew
warm, and I swished it from left
to right cheek, or pushed it up
in front of my teeth, then back
in the throat.
Mr. Woodward must have thought me
a very quiet student.
Once Judy's eyes met mine
at the wrong moment, and we giggled.
She managed to contain herself,
but my moist cargo delivered itself
all over my desk top,
and that unfortunate loss of dignity
ended the contest forever.

I can't remember
anything else I held on to,
or let go of,
in the fifth grade.   ✿

My Father Rings the Bells

On Christmas Eve
we went to bed early,
daring morning to come
with its burden of packages.
On Christmas Eve,
snuggled under the covers,
we giggled and waited.
It always came after dark,
starting out low,
getting closer and louder
until we were certain—
Santa's bells
just outside our window!
But of course we knew
whose hand shook forth
the music,
whose game announced
the future,
told us it was good,
would surely come,
would be enough.   ✵

Superior

"The value, Nancy,
of precise mechanical expertise
is that I *know*
what might go wrong next.
This trip it will probably be
the battery
or the brake fluid lines.
My knowledge allows me
to worry specifically,
whereas your worries
are all general,"
said Harold to me
on the Caranavi road.　　⊛

Fau Paux

nails scrape roof
heel jams passageway
knobs crowd crannies
and I wish I'd washed it first

awkward
this mouthful
of foot　　⊛

On Catching Frogs

(Written with the help of David and Kristin)

Well, first of all you get a jar
    and put lake water in it
    and rocks and grass in it, too

Then the frog

You have to sneak up on it
    carefully and silently
    when its back is toward you
    and it's looking the other way

    and then POP!
    (but don't squish it)
    (if you squish it
    it will make a huge mess of blood
    and you will not want it)

Then hold it very carefully
    in your wet hands
    but not too much
    or it will get hot and die

And how you know the difference
    between a frog and a rock
    is this—
    if you catch a rock, it's hard
    if you catch a frog, it's squishy

The problem is, some frogs are poison
    and how you know
    if you got a poison frog
    is this—
    you die,
    but then you don't really know
    'cause you're already dead

The best place to catch frogs
    is a slow lake
    around the edges

And the reason you catch them
    is to see how they work
    or pollywogs, to see them
    turn into frogs

I can't think of anymore now
    but if I do
    I'll let you know.   ✤

Fifteen

The year Kristin turned fifteen
we moved to Calacoto.
Her upstairs bedroom faced
the neighbor's house where
Carlos, seventeen,
sat on his second-floor balcony
looking over the hedge at her.
Sometimes Carlos strummed a guitar
and sang old Paul Anka songs—
"You are my destiny," or
"Oh, please, stay by me, Kristina,"
substituting my daughter's name
for that of the famous Diana.
Carlos' father, an obscure
but important colonel in the Bolivian army,
wasn't home much
but his maid prowled the garden
watching Carlos watching Kristin
while I watched her father
watching Carlos watching Kristin.
Kristin just sat on her bed,
petting her hamster and smiling.   ✺

After Twenty Years

It's not so much that
once-upon-a-time
you happened to me
as it is that
you keep on happening,
not so much that then
I fell-in-love
as that
I'm still living
in the hole
I fell into
and that
the view
from up here
is so expansive.

Secret Scholar

the maintenance man
in my apartment complex
is working on his ph.d. in anthropology
he unplugs drains
    like the time my garbage disposal
    wouldn't work for two weeks
    and started stinking
    I was afraid to test it
    afraid to stick my hand down
    but he fixed it
    in ten minutes
he hangs towel racks and doors
relights the pilot under water heaters
he studies the natives as he works
making secret observations
to record in his notebook
he has dirt in his knuckles
and eyes that see
more than drains   ✸

On the Road to Samaipata

"The essence of a hole is the absence of thingness,"
I said to Hal after the big bounce.

"That's profound," he replied.

"On the other hand, can the essence of anything
be the absence of another thing?"

"Good question."

"That would be a very insubstantial essence."

"Indeed. Can you think of some examples?"

"Grief? Loneliness?" I suggested.

"Or matter and antimatter."

"There you go."

I peeled a tangerine.
As we talked we ate the sweet slices,
spit the seeds out the window.   ✵

Everlasting

Long a connoisseur of the commonplace,
I flick cathedrals like lint from my sleeve.
Scholarly tomes slip-slide through the cracks
in my mind, leaving no trace.
Monuments (cheap, plentiful, easy to construct)
I erase from memory without compunction.

But the way you look at me
burrows deep, sequoia thick.
Your slightest touch leaves an indelible mark.
The lights in your voice are forever.   �֎

Both of Us
Have Never
Been
Nuns

Guided Tour

Just follow me, folks,
and keep on the path.
To our right here
we have a genuine tree.
Note its separate parts—
branches, stems, twigs, leaves.
The thickness in the center
is called trunk.
It is covered with bark—
its skin, so to speak.
Off there in the distance
to your left is ocean.
The big blue thing
that sort of shivers.
Archeologists tell us
it has been around
for a very long time,
although carbon-dating
has not seemed to help
in determining its
exact age.

And here below us
at our very feet
if you will bend down
and look closely—
I give you sand.
Composed of many
tiny particles,
each with its unique
and private geometry,
it is an example of
raw, natural
unity in diversity.
I'd ask you, out of respect,
not to step on it,
but that would be quite futile
as you can see.
Now follow me.
Just around the bend
other wonders await us—
stones, sky, squirrels,
and maybe, if the timing
is right, a dandelion
will roar.   ✳

I Am Popular

with dogs & babies
meaning
individuals
from those groups
tend to like me
right
off
the bat
without even
knowing
my credentials.

If they
could vote
I'd win
the election
to whatever
office I
was running
for.

As far as
popularity
per se
goes
I can live
with that.

One could
do worse
than
be liked
by

dogs & babies.   ✾

Footnote to History

In spite of his literary legacy—
Declaration of Independence,
Notes on the State of Virginia,
and 20,000 letters
now catalogued
under glass. . .

Regardless of his two-term
presidency in the youth
of our nation. . .

Notwithstanding the genius
that crafted and constructed
a Monticello. . .

And overlooking his botanical
gifts to Virginia—the Oregon
snow berry bush, South
African geranium,
a golden rain tree from
somewhere in Asia—

Thomas Jefferson died a pauper,
estate auctioned, slaves sold
south, family scattered.

"He wrote down each and every
penny he spent," the lecturer
informs. "I'm not sure he
added them up."   ✦

Ralph

Although the canon is closed
and somewhere there's a warning
against adding to Holy Writ

i had a dream last night
in which it was revealed to me
that the unnamed leper in

Luke
had a name
that his name was

Ralph
that he lived with his mother
who never touched him

who ran a pickle business
on the corner of 42nd and Main
in downtown Jerusalem

who had a big nose
and yelled lots
yelled at Ralph

which didn't help
his self-esteem
low anyway what with

leprosy spots and losing limbs
and i know it will cost a lot of money
to recall all those Bibles

from all those bookstores
in all those midwestern towns
but it has to be done

because this is important information
needed for exegesis
and because i feel certain

Ralph would have wanted it this way.   ✿

Tutorial

("It is the task of science to systemize the fuzziness of its objects of inquiry, not to ignore it or argue it away."
—Robert de Beaugrande and Wolfgang Dressler)

Like soldiers on parade
my arguments stood in rank and file,
at attention,
boots polished, medals shining,
faces stern.
That was yesterday.
Today I ask
where did this fuzz come from?
Fuzz on their uniforms,
fuzz smearing their medals,
fuzz growing out their ears
and nostrils.
The edges have blurred.
What will the general say?   ⊛

Writing the Dissertation

like squeezing melons
through a narrow-necked bottle
>   *

I write things like
>   missiologically communicative text
>   global discourse structure
>   fragmentation/integration dichotomy
then look in the mirror
to see who's saying that stuff
>   *

pretending smart
no longer worrying pretty
missing funny
>   *

No ledges break the face of this mountain.
I inch skyward, not daring to look down,
praying the ropes hold.
>   *

writing a sick sentence
editing out what little life there was
blowing the ashes off the page
starting over
>   *

Both of Us Have Never Been Nuns

The endless re-writing,
the pushing, poking, pulling.
I wonder if I'll end up
with a wingless butterfly collection,
rows of tiny thoraxes of thought.

    *

I hope no one institutionalizes me
but I've been talking to myself
a lot lately. Sometimes I answer back.

    *

Right now "The Little Engine That Could"
is better than the Bible.

    *

wondering what any of this
has to do with life

    *

dreaming of a time with
no abstracts no footnotes
no references cited no indexes
ever again ✲

An Ecumenical Quaker Draws the Line

Can't say I'm not open.
I meditate with Mennonites,
chant with Catholics,
and belt out Baptist blues with the best of them.
I danced at my daughter's wedding to a Nazarene,
and once I even rolled the aisle with a Pentecostal.
But with funerals I reach my limit.
When my time comes
I will insist on my own homespun,
tried and true Quaker version.
I just wouldn't feel dead
without it.   ❀

Some Input, Please!

After a time
of withsitting and outthinking
all of this,
I've decided I've had
enough of your roundtalk.
Straightpoint me to the facts.
Give me input
or I shall take
my wherewithall,
upget,
and outgo. ✵

Zoology Lesson

Rare and amazing bird, the rhinoceros.
With much effort and scant grace, she lifts off,
a leathery B-2 bomber, horn into the wind,

third cousin to the unicorn, though much removed.
Aerodynamically sub-standard, she is living miracle,
a giant bumblebee without the buzz. With quiet

dignity she lumbers through the African skies,
tearing clouds, bruising the sunset, a marvel
to behold. Who could believe it?

Advice for those who find themselves in the vicinity
of a flying rhinoceros: Never laugh. A rhinoceros
takes herself seriously and expects you to do

likewise. Never scorn the lowly buffalo bird on her back.
He is there by invitation, a first-class passenger,
built-in siren and parasite disposal system; he is a

friend that sticketh closer; such devotion in any
context is rare; respect is his due. Never stand in
an open field when a rhinoceros is flying overhead.   ⊛

A Real Poem

(Once at a poetry reading, a man named Albert asked me why my poetry didn't rhyme. Real poetry, he informed me, rhymes. This is a poem for Albert.)

Roses are red
violets are cruel
if you don't behave
I'll send you to school
for the rest of your life
and you won't ever marry
or sleep with a wife.

Sugar is sweet
but bad for your teeth
when you go outdoors
put on your sneeth
and don't forget
to breathe through your nose
and don't play with daggers
or take off your clothes.

The love of mother
is greater by far
than the love of fudge
or snake or bar
and what a wonder

what a marvelous thing
is the gift of laughter
and the overwhelming serendipitous
    ability of the human race to sing.

Sunsets are golden
moonrise is blue
taffy is daffy
and so are you
one two
buckle your shoe
when you walk on the grass
don't step in the pooh
pray at all times
but don't sneeze when you do
sneezing's irreverent
your prayers won't come true.

Praise the wonder of onions
the blessing of sleep
the yipping of puppies
the bleating of sheep
the glory of starlight
chicks that go peep
cabbage in springtime
and poems when they're deep.   ✿

Both of Us Have Never Been Nuns

Conversation with Mike on Religion

Nancy, are you the one
who used to be a nun?

> No. I've never been a nun.
> What about you?

I've never been a nun either.

> What a coincidence. Both of us
> have never been nuns.

Small world.

> And to think Ferdinand thought
> it was flat. But he changed
> his mind when Columbus
> showed him an egg.

That'll do it every time.

A Word Like Lugubrious

needs a poem of its own.
Consider the slime and the slink of it,
the slightly sinister wink of its eye
as it peeks from behind potted plants at wakes,
lingers at the altars of Protestant revivals,
or sobs with soap opera heroines.
An irreverent Uriah Heapish word,
a marbles-in-the-mouth sound,
it offers no apologies
for its lumpish singularity.

Some suggestions for everyday use:
—"This piano is lugubriously out of tune."
—"He shed a lugubrious tear
    as she passed him the marmalade."
—"This morning at exactly 5:37,
    a lugubrious lummox was sighted
    at the corner of 11th and Lucerne
    in downtown L.A. We have investigators
    on the scene and will interrupt our broadcast
    to bring up-to-date coverage
    on this fast-breaking story."
—"Not tonight, dear. I'm feeling lugubrious."   ⊛

Overheard in an "Experienced Car Lot"

So what
if my paint is chipped
and the right front door won't open?
There's a knowing air
about me
a kind of rightness
in having bumped before
over country roads.
My ends are not
yet exhausted.
The mellowed wisdom
that eddies from my eyes
will show as much of the way
on a dark night
as you need to know.
The rattle in my song
is well worth noting
and all my joints
are universal.　　⊛

Sign on the Grand Canyon Trail

When mules pass stand quietly.
Don't whisper, shuffle or sigh.
If the breeze is right
you might catch it
on the edge of memory—
mules humming the ancient song.

When mules pass stand quietly.
Avert your gaze.
It's rude to stare
and dangerous too,
like looking into the sun
reflected in a beetle's eye.
Focus on the far wall of the canyon,
on the inevitable rainbow,
the distant storm.
Pretend you don't see.

When mules pass stand quietly
and follow the mule guide's instructions—
the hand signals, the cryptic glances.
Be silent and sin not.
Mules are passing.
The moment is holy.   ✾

Both of Us Have Never Been Nuns

A Mouse Ate My Poem

and I'm really mad.
It had been months since the words flowed
from brain to hand to page and I was anguished,
wondering if my muse was on an extended coffee break
or if this was a clear-cut case of abandonment.
But then, last night as I was brushing my teeth,
it came to me, pure and full-blown, the perfect poem.
So I rushed from the bathroom to my desk,
grabbed paper and pen, put it all down,
then basked for a moment in creative relief.
I left it there on the edge where I'd be sure
to see it first thing in the morning.

It's morning now, but all I find are nibbled margins,
a few Sanskrit footprints in the dust,
    and down on the carpet,
barely visible, one small grey poop of a metaphor. ⊛

The Key Is Fish Lips

I have this puzzle—
an under-the-ocean fantasy cartoon
in rainbow hues, crystal clear
with no muck at all.
All kinds and colors mingle
and no one is eating anyone else.
It's nice to know that's how it is
on the bottom of the ocean
'cause it's sure not like that up here.
There's lots of muck where I live
and the mingling gets complicated.
The perfect scene on the box lid
is all in tiny pieces on my table,
but I've discovered the key
for bringing it together. It's fish lips.
Amazing things, coming as they
do in such variety—some thinly protruding,
others smushed into the cheeks.
Some pouting, others ready for a big fish
kiss. I now have a little pile of fish lips
and, using the box lid as guide,

I place them just so on the table.
Little by little the rest of each fish
follows, not wanting
to be separated for long from its lips.
Then the background fills in—kelp,
bubbles, rays of sunlight. Soon
it's all one—harmonious and whole.
I come away from the table renewed
in hope, knowing that the pieces
of my life will also one day come together,
and that for it to happen all I have to do
is first find the fish lips.   ⊛

Entering
the
Forest

After the Coup

The neighbors peer through drawn curtains,
antennae quivering.
Across town a lone car pushes beetle-like uphill,
the only movement marring a steel-life fantasy.
The taut air hums a high thin song
beyond the threshold of silence.
Tanks like ironclad kittens hide,
crouched and ready.
Suspended in this moment,
the city waits.   ✳

On Committing Fatal Error 500

While floating through cyberspace,
attempting to locate and land on
any friendly planet,
I committed
Fatal Error 500
(not 100, 54, 176, or 329).
Am I now condemned to a living death,
spinning in an unconnected void?
Dizzy, drunk on my own failure,
I don't know how to rebuild my desktop,
much less my life.
Is there a savior on the netscape?
Is there a way home?   ✳

Church Service

No ceiling fan
can simulate a breeze
    when the windows are shut
and the air   heavy with hyperbole.

Our packs are far too light,
the ascent a game;
    who can find the trail
in such a fog?   ❀

A Reasonable Request

Don't bother us, God.
We paid our dues three centuries ago
    with George Fox, Elizabeth Fry, James Naylor
    and all those martyrs.
There's blood on our records
    if not on our limbs.

We're exempt now
    not only from taxes
    but from forced labor in difficult places
    and all forms of suffering
    and/or persecution.

We've become a strictly non-prophet organization. ❀

Evangelist at the Sheraton

The carpet spreads red and purple
in the vast field of the convention hall.
Many pronged chandeliers bloom overhead,
giant dandelion puffballs.

Do they swing slightly in the wind of God's Anointed?

> *"JESUS! JESUS! LIVES!*
> *AND HE'S HERE! HERE!*
> *NOWOWOWOWOWOWOWOWOWOWowowwowowowow."*

The audience moans and sways
and I, trapped, look up
and wonder—
what if all the blowing and bellowing
shook those spikes of light
to their skinny roots, broke them loose
and tumbled them earthward?
What would they sow for tomorrow?
Would hundreds of little yellow chandeliers
sprout up from the carpet
in some fantastic harvest of rebirth
come spring?   ✿

Coming of Age

"It's all right," he assured me
as his ear slid
slowly
down the side
of his face.
His right index finger dropped
off
next.
He had always
known this would happen
someday.
His hairline had begun
to recede
years before.
We walked out of
the room
single
file.

I stumbled on
his left
foot.
He hobbled ahead,
scattering appendages
like
bread
crumbs.
About twilight
we entered the forest.　　⊛

Entering the Forest

45

The Leader

He comes The Leader with much applause
and turning of heads and scraping
and bring out the candles and celebrity damask!
(Color the carpet red,
the ride first-class,
the bills paid.
Color His face smiley in the morning papers.)
For He's here our great our only
our venerated Christian VIP!
So spread the banquet rich and pungent
and politely munch and listen
to His poised and perpendicular words
on world poverty the whole man
healing helping loving feeding
(please pass the shrimp cocktail).
Render to Him His due acclamation.
    And meanwhile gently ignore the other—
the servant the sufferer the lowly lamb
watching in sorrow from behind
the potted geraniums.   ✻

The Haircut

What can one say
to a woman named Madge
with orange hair and huge hands
who says, "Take off your glasses
and relax,"
then rises in the mirror
like a full moon,
omniscient, regal,
and plies her trade?　❀

Manners

You look at me
as I speak
and nod at the right times
saying pleasantly,
"Is that so?
How interesting!"
Your tone is well modulated,
your manner impeccable,
your attention appropriately rapt.
Clearly, you have developed
the art of listening.

But nothing, friend,
can disguise
the yawn
I see in your eyes.   ✿

My Friend Crowley

knows things like
where on the stem to cut the rose,
which breakfast cereals are truly organic,
who the modern prophets are, and all
the secret names of the Holy Spirit.
Crowley knows this stuff
and much more.
He's generous with his insights.
He sends his word warriors out
on a thin path. Sleek and brown,
they crouch as they run. Their arrows are hand
hewn, sharp, sure as death.
It's wise to agree with Crowley,
affirm his positions and opinions
with a nod, a grunt, an intelligent glint in the eye.
He likes to know that you know that
he knows.   ✻

It Happened One Night

I was asleep in my room
the night the Department of Human Resource
Management lost control.
I woke to a riot of sounds.
Out in the street hundreds
of human resources ran amok,
tripping over unleashed
goal statements and reassessment plans.
Outcomes clashed with means,
and although no blood was shed
—human resources not having any—
the stench of unrealized potential
filled the land.
By morning the beeping
of a single cell phone
was all that broke the silence.
The human resources, I suppose,
were back under control,
leaving only us people
to find our way
through the maze
as best we can.   ✿

From
Bolivian
Mud

Prayer from the Plane

Lord,
we're almost there.
The plane's losing altitude,
> and from the window
> I see Lake Titicaca.

This is hard to believe
> after the months of preparation,
> of dreams and plans.

> And now the reality.
> Missionaries at last.

But I'll have to confess, Lord,
> joy isn't my only emotion.

> I'm afraid.

In the excitement of the rallies back home,
> everyone telling us what a great thing we were doing
> and how much they would pray,
> and among the crowd seeing us off at the Portland
> > Airport,

> it was easy to feel
> like a conquering warrior in your missionary army.
> Nothing too difficult and the nations to win!

From Bolivian Mud

But now, Lord, the crowds and rousing songs are gone.
    Just Hal, David and I
    wait for the plane to land.
    And we three alone will step off onto Bolivian ground.

We three—and you.
    There's our hope.

I'm afraid, Lord.
    Take my hand.
    Be my guide in this new land.
    I don't know what's ahead—
    just that you'll be there with me.
    Let my expectations and experiences
    be grounded
    in your reality.   ✸

From One in Shock

Lord,
I honestly thought I was prepared for culture shock.
>   After reading *Customs and Cultures* and all those
>   other anthropology books,
>   wouldn't you think I'd be a little more immune?

Tonight I went to an Aymara wedding.
>   We got there a half-hour late which offended no one.
>   The ceremony started an hour later
>   and seemed to last several more hours.
>   But it didn't really bother me until the wedding feast.
>   We walked down to the small church basement
>   and crowded together, all 300 of us, on the wooden
>   benches.

The first course was soup—hot and spicy.
>   One hour later someone
>   gave me a plate heaped full of potatoes
>   with a piece of chicken on top—the main course.
>   Those funny potatoes all stuck to the roof of my
>   mouth
>   and I could not finish.
>   All the while street odors wafted in the window
>   and mixed with the smells in front of me.

From Bolivian Mud

Lord,

    it took an effort to keep back the tears.

    This isn't my home.

    I'm not like these people.

    How can they sit there ignoring those smells?

    And how can they laugh

    crowded together in that dank dirty room?

Remind me of yourself, Lord.

    You, too, left a far country to walk among people
        different from yourself.

    You lived in simple rooms, fought dirt, drank
        unboiled water,

    smelled the same human smells that filled that room.

    Was Galilean food strange to your palate—

    you who were accustomed to food from the tree
        of life?

    Did you experience culture shock?

Remind me of this often, Lord.

    And remind me of your reason for leaving home
        to live among us.

    With you beside me, I'll rise above these feelings

    and grow into love.

    And someday—learn to laugh with them.   ⊛

Tomato Judgment

In the restaurant today
    I ordered tomato judgment
    rather than tomato juice.
    They don't sound that different in Spanish.
    My co-workers laughed, and I did, too,
    but I felt embarrassed.

    And it's not as though this were an isolated incident.

All of a sudden, speaking Spanish is no longer a game,
    a classroom drill, or a vocabulary list
    to master for tomorrow's quiz.

    It's life.

All those people walking down the street
    buy, sell, play, work, write letters,
    sing songs, read newspapers, flirt, curse,
    and tell jokes in Spanish!
    In perfect, effortless Spanish!
    Even the kids
    jabber away like linguistic experts.
    I can conjugate "decir" better than they can,
    and explain where in the mouth the "g" sound is formed,
    but can I order a simple glass of tomato juice?

From Bolivian Mud

For friendship to happen,
    I need to be warm and spontaneous.
    Yet how is that possible
    when I have to mentally coax every phrase
    before it has the nerve to creep out my mouth?

Patience, I'm told.
    Just have patience, practice lots
    and keep laughing at yourself.

    Guess I'll have to, Lord.
    Everyone else is.   ✹

A Prayer from Mom

Lord,

Hal and I took David with us
to the weekend conference in the valley.
It was good to share as a family in your work,
to travel, meet people and places together.
Even rough it together.
Thank you that David adjusts so well to new situations.

But, Lord, raising my children in another culture
isn't going to be easy.
A few incidents this past weekend pointed that out.
On Saturday, for example,
David wanted to play in the dirt. Fine. A normal
   boy desire.
But as he sat down the village children crowded around,
attracted by his fair skin and blond hair.
All the kids wanted to pat his head, tell him how cute
   he was,
hand stones to him.
He was literally the center of an admiring circle.

And, Lord, every lady at that conference had to hold him,
many of them telling him how much nicer he was
than their "common brown children."
And in front of their children!

From Bolivian Mud

59

I realize that part of my job as a mother
  is to help David develop a good self image.
  But really, Lord, isn't this going a bit far?
  Will he grow up thinking himself the center of the
    universe?
  What will happen when he goes home
  and finds no admiring throngs?

Lord,
  I need your wisdom.
  Help me as I guide this child.
  Let him grow up with a proper perspective of himself,
  of the world and his relationship to it.
  Let him learn to give his attention to others,
  not expecting them to admire his every move.
  Let him learn to love.

Be in me as I am his first example in all of this.

And every day, Lord Jesus,
  remind me that I am a mother
  before I am a missionary.   ✷

Exit Alice, Enter Tom

Kristin cut her hair today, Lord.
David rushed into the kitchen,
ever ready to inform me
of his sister's latest misadventure.
"Mommy! O Mommy!
You ought to see what Kristin's done now!
She's really ugly!"

I whispered your name, Lord,
and ran to the bedroom,
visions of bloody limbs and painted faces
racing before me.

She was standing in the middle of the room,
scissors in hand,
two small piles of blond hair at her feet
and a wistful half-smile tugging at her mouth.
A real waif.

I started to scold,
but burst out laughing.
Gone—my long-haired vision of Alice-in-Wonderland,
my delicate princess.

From Bolivian Mud

Hal finished the job,
and now she looks like the Tom-boy
she really is.
I miss her long golden hair,
but Kristin is still Kristin.

Which leaves me wondering—what next?

From Bolivian Mud

Lord God Almighty, Powerful King,
    Maker and Mover of mountains
    and universes,
we're stuck in a river.
We've been here for over an hour
    and what I want to know is—
    why don't you get us out?
Sure, the scenery is great,
    but I'll bet it's just as pretty
    'round the bend.
Those mountains—
    you raised them up from nothing
    with a mere creative word.
Why are you mute now?
Speak, Lord, and resurrect this hunk
    of steel, fiberglass and rubber
    from its muddy grave.
Move, miracle worker, feeder of 5,000,
    elemental wine maker, curer,
    creator.
I know you can do it.
After all, I'm here on your business.

But here I sit.

Could it be
    you're trying to tell me something,
    something I can only hear
    from this river bed?
Could it be
    you have your reasons and lessons
    and character sessions
    better learned mid-stream
    than mid-church service?

OK, Lord,
    I give in.
Pardon my griping
    and teach me
    what I need to know.
In all of this
    I'm still your
    wet but
    willing servant.

All Creatures

"All things wise and wonderful,
All creatures great and small,
All things bright and beautiful,
The Lord God made them all."

I like that song, Lord, really I do.
But the part about all creatures,
the great and the small—
is it true? All of them?
Did you, Lord, make amoeba?
And if so, why?

Neither wise, wonderful, bright nor beautiful,
they have burrowed themselves
into my son's liver
and if you're behind this—
what do you intend to do about it?

We've been through numerous rounds of Flagil,
tried some potent "natural" remedies,
all mixed with generous dosages of prayer,
and now I'm ready for some answers.

From Bolivian Mud

Are these particular little beasts
part of some vast incredible Plan,
hatched in the heavenly imagination
since before the foundations
and all that?

Do they have a role like Jonah's feisty worm,
a place in the Great Dance,

or are they jitterbugging in my son's insides
just for the fun of it?

This is ridiculous, isn't it, Lord—
    red-faced me shaking my fist
    at the Creator of all creatures great and small.

    Forgive me. I know I'm absurd.
    But I'm also scared.

    I have a feeling you can take my rage
    and still go on loving me.

But please, if these things belong to you,
    provide some other place for them
    to make their beds and cook their soup
    and do their dances

    so David can stop doing his.   ✦

On Skipping Rocks

They say Business Meetings are important,
    but must they be so unpleasant, Lord?
    While you show us the Big Picture,
    couldn't you also fill us in on more of the details?
    Reports, budgets, strategies, and decisions
    took the better part of the last two days.
    We discussed difficult issues and disagreements
        surfaced.
    My neck ached from the tension.

Today we drove out to a border town on the lake
    to meet with our Peruvian colleagues.
    The Andes, snowcapped and shining, lined up
    like sentinels against the brilliant blue of
        Lake Titicaca,
    but this time I hardly even noticed, Lord.
    Yesterday's discussion rode with us and,
    like bugs on the windshield, riveted my attention.

From Bolivian Mud

Once on the border, another meeting took up most of the
    afternoon.
    Afterwards, choked up with the solemnity of Mission
    Business,
    I escaped to the lake shore
    where the kids were engaged
    in the serious business of play.
    The lake and the breeze were doing a subtle ballet
    under a grey afternoon sky.
    Dark and light tones advanced and changed places,
    gliding like living taffeta.
    I walked along the edge, savoring the silence.

David offered to teach me the art of skipping rocks.
    You've got to practice, he informed me,
    because skipping rocks is important.
    A nine bouncer tells you you're really someone.
    I only made it to four bounces,
    but even that felt good.

I then threw a handful of pebbles into the water
and the sound was wonderful—a concert of plops,
a good grey music.
Soon all the kids were doing it.
I said, "Go!" and we all tossed at once.
Then, of course, everyone had to have a turn saying "Go."
After each performance, we burst out laughing.
Could Mozart have done better?

That was the best part of a long week.
I stopped taking myself and The Work so seriously.
Once again, I saw the mountains, heard the wind,
felt trust that you will resolve all those difficult issues.
And more, I was able to return, face my co-workers,
and know that I love them.

Lord, give me rock skipping moments every day. ✽

From Bolivian Mud

Declaration

Lord, my rights are being violated again—
    my God-inspired, law-defended,
    historically battled, humanly holy
    constitutional rights
and it's not fair!
I'm doing my share of the work
    carrying my part of the load
    and now
    they want to give me their shares—
    want me to go the extra mile their
        legs refuse to walk,
    and I'm mad.

But when I stop and think
    —let your Spirit in through the chinks
    in the door (boarded fast by rights)—
    I'm even more bothered
    by my strong
    attachment to this sense of
    what's-fair-for-me.

Did you have rights, too, Lord?
Where were they when you left
   your home
   to walk and eat and love
   among us? when you left the green fields
   of glory to wander our dusty roads
   and teach us giving and losing as
   a superior form of gain?
Where were your rights when you
   hung there high in the afternoon?
Was it fair for you to carry
   the weight of a world full of
   people like me?
Was it right?

Forgive me, Lord.
In the light of your life
   I begin to see my rights
   more clearly.
Untie these knots that bind me
   in my fight for fairness.
Free me to give and lose and carry more
   than my share.
Help me to forget my rights
   and enter into love.   ✿

From Bolivian Mud

71

The Spare

It's happened again.
I knew it would.
But it was working out so well—
   brown with brown,
   blue tube with blue tube,
   two whites with red rings,
   and all the others
when down at the bottom of the basket
I saw it,
   an unobtrusive
   but obviously spare
   sock.
No mate.
I can't use it unless it's connected.
Throwing it away would be wasteful.
After all, who knows
when the other one will show up?
Why is there always one spare sock
on laundry day?

I feel like a spare sock tonight, Lord.
I'm not sure of my place or function.
I'm unconnected, ill at ease
and feeling guilty about it.

Everyone else seems to know
who they are
and where they belong,
and I,
I'm misplaced,
useless
 (though in no imminent danger
 of being thrown away)
and lonesome.

Match me up, Lord.
Unite me again with
your purpose and plan.
Show me my place
and, please,
give a hint of a promise
that someday
all the parts and pieces
will fit.   ❀

From Bolivian Mud

Custom Designed

Lord, I applaud You!
>How intricate your creation!
>I'm coming to believe you custom design people
>to match the place you put them in.

Take the Aymara woman.
>I spent the weekend with 300 of them
>in a women's conference on the altiplano,
>Bolivia's high windy plateau.

We spent lots of time sitting in meetings.
>Aymara country women don't sit on benches.
>They squat on blankets laid on the ground.
>I tried it.
>All weekend long I tried it,
>wanting to be one with them,
>not "La Señora Misionera,"
>set apart on her chair in the front.

But I know now, Lord, that you constructed those women
>differently than you did me.
>They can sit in one position for hours,
>serene, happy, nursing their babies
>or amening the sermon,

looking as though they naturally
grew up out of the ground—
a living part of it.

Me? Well, first I crossed my legs
under my long quilted skirt.
After a while I stretched my limbs out in front,
then I folded them to the left,
then I rubbed them awake and switched to the right.
After that I started the cycle again.
I fidgeted and twitched and ached the whole weekend.

But they didn't.

I'm amazed at these ladies, Lord,
not only at how comfortable they are
sitting on the ground,
but at how they seem built to defy the cold and wind,
to roll with life in this high stark place.
Short and rounded,
bundled in their layers of bright skirts and shawls,
they make me think of living Easter eggs,
meeting the challenge of the altiplano
with spunk and color.

Sunday afternoon the conference ended

From Bolivian Mud

and the ladies dispersed,
walking the kilometers back to their own villages.
Every direction I looked
green, red, purple, yellow and blue Easter eggs
floated out over the prairie,
gradually becoming smaller and smaller,
points of color peppering the planes,
dots of light,
the spectrum of your love.

How wonderful your craftsmanship, Lord!
How intricate your designs!   ✺

Joyful Noise

Arturo is preaching now.
 The Aymara gutturals and rasps pour out
 and fill this small adobe building
 with admonitions from your word.
 Staccato rain fists
 beat their rhythm on the tin roof.
 It doesn't seem to bother the preacher at all.

 Other noises mingle to form a background music—
 the yip of a drenched dog outside the window,
 from time to time a baby's cry,
 quickly smothered in mother's breast,
 the various rustlings, scuffings and turnings
 of the people gathered here to worship you.

 An altiplano wind whips around the building,
 rattling the windows, but here inside,
 200 crowded bodies keep the cold from distracting.
 I wrap my poncho tighter around me
 and enjoy the sounds.

Earlier, five musical groups took turns to praise,
 accompanied by flutes, guitars and one incongruous drum.
 The congregation swayed, clapped and joined in,
 moved by the beat and the simple words.

From Bolivian Mud

77

The storm outside is getting louder.
Arturo just finished his sermon
    and the congregation is shifting forward and to their knees.
    Your people explode into pleas and wails and high-pitched
        praises,
    outdoing the rain.
    I visualize the praying, a living block of sound,
    rising and coming before you,
    a bright and holy gift.

Thank you, Lord, for the exuberance of my brothers and sisters.
Thank you that this joyful noise mixes with heaven's own music.
Thank you that in any form or language, our praises please you.
And thank you for showing me that this boisterous place of pray
    is a temple of the living God.   ❀

The Image

So much is expected of me, Lord.
It's as though the name "missionary"
 carries a halo that I'm
 supposed to shove my head under
 even if it doesn't fit.
And Lord—it doesn't.

Sure, I can pretend—
 be like a peacock
 parading spiritual plumage,
 strutting and fanning
 my gorgeous statistics
 and souvenirs
 before an admiring audience

 polish the image—
 my special brand of holiness.

 I can hide behind
 my maps and slides and foreign sounds,
 win approval,
 maybe even admiration.

From Bolivian Mud

And if I work it right
    they'll never know
        about the churches we lost to heresy,
        the bickering among the
        national brethren
    never guess
        the loneliness and frustration
        the crowded afternoons when
        my sanctification slips.

They'll never know, never guess—
    if I don't tell them.

Or should I tell?

So much is expected of me, Lord.
And I get tired of it.
I've lain in this mold so long
    I almost fit,
    and that scares me.

Help me.
Help me crack the image.
Help me dare to be real.   ❊

More Than a Jelly Bean

It happened during worship service.
    "Come to the rally, ladies,"
    the leader chimed with platform cheer.
    "Nancy Thomas will be speaking
    and I know it'll be a real treat!"

I cringed as I heard that, Lord,
    and scrunched up in my seat.
    Into my brain popped the picture
    of a huge green jelly bean,
    propped against the pulpit,
    all the ladies leaning forward,
    tongues hanging out.
    A real treat.

Lord, I don't want to be a treat, real or otherwise!
    What does a jelly bean have to offer?
    A colored globe of gelled sugar,
    it stains the tongue and gums up the hands.
    No food value.
    Who'd give jelly beans to feed the poor?

From Bolivian Mud

Oh, Lord, am I sometimes just a treat?
Were you speaking to me
in that clumsy announcement?
Are there times when I
speak/teach/write/mother/encourage
—even do it well—
in my own strength?
Could it be whenever I'm too busy to wait on you,
to consciously draw life from your Spirit,
I end up offering jelly beans
instead of food?

Forgive me, Lord.
I know that without you I can do nothing,
no matter how busy or successful.

Draw me close.
Let your Spirit so fill me
that, like Jesus, I do what I see the Father doing,
speak what I hear the Father saying.

Please, Lord,
make me more than a jelly bean.

A Psalm for Public Speakers

I will extol the Lord

Before the people
    I will show his worth
    and works

With humor I will speak of
    his surprises
    his seeming sleight-of-hand
    his naturalness
    his delightful rabbit-out-of-hat
        grace moments

I will not construct word scaffolding
    on my behalf
    make-shift efforts to bolster
    my reputation
I will not strain to hide
    my clownishness
    behind eloquence
        the neatness of introduction-threepoints-conclusion
        the cleverness of rhyme and rhythm

From Bolivian Mud

83

I will not push
for applause
popularity
or acclaim

but
I will

(with ease and aplomb
with trippings and bumblings)

I will
I will
I will

extol the Lord.　⊛

Confession

I know now, Lord,
that I am superfluous,
that the onward march
of your kingdom
does not depend on
my small measure
of faith or talent,
that your mighty church
will grow and win and
overcome whether or not I do.
No angels stand in the wings
breathlessly watching
my performance,
knowing that my words or acts
are pivotal. No heavenly history
books record my battles and declarations.
I stand barren
before you, the sovereign God
who could defeat hell's battalions
with a mere word (as, in fact,
you did), accomplish your mission
without my ant-army efforts.

From Bolivian Mud

Yet, Lord, you choose to use me,
choose to empower these hands
to plant and water a growing church,
to demonstrate your glory through
a series of single superfluous smallnesses.
In my days of accomplishment,
remind me again of my emptiness
without you and that the fruit these hands
yield is from you.
Sheer bounty.

A Psalm for High Places

Where Poems Begin

*(Written on the freeways between
Pasadena and San Bernardino)*

1

In the times between poems
I always wonder where,
when, and if the next one will come.
My mind is a desert.
No hints of clouds.
Not even a breeze.

2

Traffic on the 10—
thick medicine down a child's throat.
A clogged river, logs bumping,
frogs too nervous to jump
or even croak.
The slow birth of an overdue baby.
Extruded metal, white-hot, lethal.
An hour glass, one grain at a time,
and me in the dentist's chair.

A Psalm for High Places

3

Poems come

from an old photograph in my purse—Tom and Becky
   grinning, me angry at some childish injustice, forever
   frozen in pout

from last night's dream—holding a baby in the palm of
   my hand, forgetting to feed it, waking up with dead-
   baby grief

from the fish that swims in the periphery of vision,
   clownfaced, gills pumping, the spot just under its eye
   bright orange

from the sound of motorcycles riding the yellow bumps
   between the cars, audacious as violets

from billboards that say the toys are back new low prices
   buy the beer get the gear it's what a hamburger is all
   about

from the garbage along the shoulder—pieces of tire, bits
   of metal, impersonal leftovers from private tragedies

from quiet concentration, hand steady on the steering
   wheel

from nothing much, from everything

4

"Barbara. Barbara."
Long and low you call her name.
In the bedroom down the hall
I wake up to more darkness
than I bargained for.
"Barbara."
She's dead, Daddy,
I want to say but don't.
You wouldn't hear me,
but I hear you
across the years.
I sink in your voice.

5

Road Sign With Arrows:
Archibald Ave North ←
Archibald Ave South →

If I were to take Archibald Ave North
would I meet sea horses in yellow trousers,
houses sprouting lavender flames
and more potato chips
than my thirst will ever quench?

A Psalm for High Places

Will Alex be there? If not,
Archibald himself? I'd prefer Alex.

But if, on the ubiquitous other hand,
I should elect Archibald Ave South,
would I arrive at the Egyptian Museum
of the Dead? Who would greet me?
Would I find the great new
horizon of all graduation speeches,
or only tremors and nursing homes?

I don't know how to choose.

6

"This vehicle makes wide right turns,"
the truck ahead informs us.
Well so does this one, so watch out.
I'm thinking that, all things considered,
I'm ready for a right turn
and it will be a wide one.
This time I'm sure.   ✸

Botany Lecture

The words like petals fell
in the lecture hall
and I gathered them in my notebook.
Now I spread them on the dining
room table to dry. A scent rises

from Virginia bluebell, dwarf flag and
the marriage of tulips—Marcus Aurelius
with the Queen of the Amazon.
Lemon lily, larkspur, and honeysuckle
azalea nudge shy Sweet William.
Snowberry blooms from the Columbia
River gorge, nearly crushed
in the pockets of Lewis and Clark,
join the South African geranium and
blossoms of a golden rain
tree from somewhere in Asia.
The vanilla scent of the heliotrope
—*Its smell rewards its care*—is almost
overcome by the crown imperial lily
with roots and blooms that stink
like a skunk—*You don't want
to approach it downwind.*—
The rose relatives—apothecary, musk,
soprano, and Belmont Banshee—
brush my palms.

A Psalm for High Places

The practical vegetable and fruit families
offer tennis ball lettuce, Arkansas pea,
the cidery temptations of the Hughes crab
apple, the pink and plump Breast
of Venus peach.

I taste the sounds. The sounds taste me.
They dizzy me, drop me,
spin me around.
One continent and two centuries removed
from the gardens of Monticello,
I have nothing but the words.
The words are enough.   ✽

Time

*("Time is abstract. You can't
hear, smell, taste, feel or see it."*
—Yoshiyuki Nishioka*)*

tastes like a Bolivian mango,
I slice it from the seed,
suck juice from my fingers.

is a dragon disguised as a train,
roars down the night,
spews venom, dreams.

hides its eggs in the Andes,
shares secrets with condors,
teaches its young to glide the wind.

eats raw potatoes
without peeling them,
skin, eyes, and all.

jumps in the pond,
dog paddles to the center,
sends taffeta rings back to shore.

cross-dresses, is not picky,
leans to lavender,
but will wear all shades of salt.

smells like the bodies
of small children happy
after summer sun.

A Psalm for High Places

wears clothes loosely,
is apt to shed them
without warning.

sings in my bones
a song without words,
they do not break.

sticks to my tongue
like icy steel,
draws blood.

wears granny glasses
but frequently forgets
to put them on.

is knobbed and gnarled,
old oak or the warts
on children's feet.

holds fast the verities,
believes in dinosaurs and the Holy Ghost,
tells lies when necessary.

likes to skinny dip,
collects sea shells,
draws from a deep well.   ✸

Lydia Watches Her Language

("I have to watch my language when I'm around you."
—my friend Lydia, Huntington Gardens, June 1998*)*

The words float from her mouth
in cartoon balloons
and Lydia watches them.
They catch the wind
and bob above our heads.
Gangly adjectives
in their summer tank tops
slip-slide the air,
while verbs in all sizes and shapes
slither around the tall bushes
bordering our path
through the simulated rain forest.
"Would you look at that!"
Lydia says. I do.
A singular noun, solid, sinks
and shudders just above ground level.
"I'm amazed," she says, "I just can't
take my eyes off it."
Sometimes an unclassified word
sneaks out, hovers a moment
then explodes in mid-air
leaving purple clouds of residue
that soon disappear.

A Psalm for High Places

She loves the plant words
best of all, dipping the liquid sounds
from a bottle near her heart,
blowing through the circle
until they escape, bubbles
in seventy shades of green.
"Stamen," she says, "pistil,
photosynthesis."
They rise before our eyes,
reflect the sun, bump, burst.
No matter. There are more
where those came from.
"I could watch them forever,"
Lydia tells me.
And for the rest of the afternoon
she does.　　❀

Metamorphosis

A large lady
in a black bathing-suit
bends at her non-waist,
tucks short hair
into a rubber cap,
straightens,
approaches the surf.
A timid June bug,
an ostrich past her prime.
She frowns.
First one foot, then the other,
she enters the ocean.
The waves take her.
Grown small
she begins to bob.
She pirouettes, sashays,
does the locomotion.
Round and lovely,
she is light as helium,
graceful as God.
Seagulls applaud.   ✿

A Psalm for High Places

Off Managaha Island

(Saipan, 1998)

I hang suspended
in a world
of rainbow beasts.
They weave the water—
slivers of yellow,
zebra stripes, Moorish idols,
the blue whorls of the juvenile emperor,
parrot fish, trumpets, schools of iridescent purple.
I feel a presence
and without moving my head
gaze up to discover myself
surrounded by needlefish,
an army of thin transparent spies
keeping me under surveillance.
Sliding through the shallows
I startle three yellow angels
whose synchronized and sudden escape
in three-stooges-style
makes me laugh.
A mouthful of salt water,
their revenge.
Under the sea's surface
I learn the secret colors of God.   ✸

God at "Penguins"

Outside "Penguins"
on Citrus and Alosta,
the August evening hums with traffic.
Sitting around a polar-white metallic table,
we speak of silence and longing for God,
"as a deer pants for the water brooks."

Kids cruise the parking lot,
impressing with the volume of their stereos
and the screech of brakes.
My yogurt cone collapses,
and Beth rescues me with a dozen napkins.
The store next door announces 25% off
on all clothes, while they last.
The cinema offers a choice: *Tom & Jerry*,
Terminator II, or *I Married an Ax Murderer*.

You ask, "Does he speak into the silence,
or is the silence itself his speech?"

We wonder, sitting there at the corner
of Citrus and Alosta on warm August evening,
sharing the silence,
knowing the kingdom come.   ✸

A Psalm for High Places

To a Would-be Geologist (Turned Missionary)

To scrounge the soil and bring up rough treasure,
to extract earth's secrets from glacier and volcano,
to study the strata, measure the masses,

then line the evidence on shelves, catalogued
(agate, obsidian, soapstone, shale):
this was light to you and life. But now,

rather than rocks, you've put your dreams
on the shelf, chosen to dig on different
ground. Instead of the concreteness of

excavations, labs, and lecture halls, you wrestle
the tougher intangibles of spirit and soul.
Instead of hypotheses, you make disciples,

and the mountains you tunnel now
only faith can move. Maybe someday,
you say, you'll collect kingdom gems, classify

crystal near the throne. Perhaps. Today's obedience
treads another turf. But your labor adds living stones
to the Temple. The Rock of Ages holds you fast.   ❀

In the Beginning

And the Spirit hovered
    over the deep,
    bent toward the black,
    cherished the nothing.

The Spirit,
    a tender gardener
    protected the small possibilities
    only Deity could see,

    nourishing the seeds
    of the kingdom to come. �֍

A Psalm for High Places

Images of the Spirit

(The coast of southern Peru, 1989)

1. Fire

Fire fear sears my memories. As a child I lay awake nights watching the walls pulsate with the glow of brush fires raging out of control in the mean California hills. Like a window on hell, sensations of flames, sirens and grim newscasters swayed around the perimeters of my dreams.

I had a friend named Vera in the third grade. She moved away and returned for a visit several years later, face and arms covered with scars. Her house had burned down and she had been trapped. I saw that my fears were not without foundation. Fire destroyed. Maimed.

I feared fire—yet was drawn to it. I remember campfires on the beach—the breakers in the background drumming the sand, laughter of friends, always a guitar, hot dogs and marshmallows roasting on sticks, and at the hub, holding it all together, the fire. It wheels through my memory, and it is good.

Here at the beach house, a candle in the dark is better than electricity. A tall thin flame sways through the rooms as I walk, dances on the walls, and lights the words and worlds in my book.

> Holy Spirit,
> I fear you
> yet I love you.
> I'm drawn to you.
>
> Without
> understanding
> I invite you.
>
> Come,
> Spirit of fire,
> dangerous
> uncontrollable One.
>
> Take me,
> burn me,
> scar me for your glory
>
> then be in me
> for them
>
> a campfire on the shore
> a candle in the dark.

A Psalm for High Places

2. Dove

At some hidden signal, the pigeons in *La Plaza de Armas* rose *en masse.* Two hundred birds just lifted into the air, a huge tapestry, and began circling the plaza. Two hundred pigeons swerving in unison, racing the airways, the only sound, the fast flutter of wings. It was obvious they were at play, a holy romp of wings and grace.

Here at the shore, I never tire of watching the birds— the lumbering pelicans, the gullinules, the ducks, the egrets. I especially enjoy the gulls, the most common by number. The flight of these birds, if it would be traced by light, would reveal a grace of curves and arcs. I think of Robert Francis' poem on sea gulls—"freedom that flows in form and still is free."

And the sounds! The lonely lovely cry of the gull prods my spirit, telling me to dig deeper, look farther, stretch, knock, seek. And find.

> Holy Spirit,
> dove,
> source of song,

move in me freely
in symmetries of grace,
inner rhythm and rhyme.

Let arc intersect arc
in perfect patterns
as my work and my play
become one
become holy
become whole.

3. Wind

The gale, fanged and taloned, rushes down the darkness, devouring towers and trees in her path. As a child I huddled in bed at night, listening to the storm, hearing the creaking of the branches, the groaning of the old house, wondering if it would still be standing in the morning.

Today the breeze strums in waves and sand a gentle grace ballad. I relax, lullabied, and know I'm safe.

Yet both winds, the rage and the whisper, issue from one source and follow the same light. And for all our complicated instruments and calculations, the movements of the air remain a mystery.

> Holy Spirit,
> all gale and glory,
> storm my gates
> destroy my defenses
> force your entrance.
>
> You! hurricane holiness of God,
> move in all your mystery
> majesty might.
> Bellow/blow
> bend and break
> all useless branches
>
> remembering
> to come again
> quietly subtly
> breathing his image
> in the fields of my heart.
>
> Holy Spirit,
> wind of God,
> come.

4. Water

I remember as a child our family excursions to a small river in the foothills of the Sierra Nevadas. Tom, Becky and I were like animals set free as we hopped from boulder to boulder, splashed in shallow pools and collected innumerable pebbles (each a treasure) to be carted home. I still gravitate to rivers—Wilson River in Oregon's autumn or the Zongo River in any season. Just give me a rock to sit on and time to become silent. I'm held for hours by the sound and feel and smell and spirit of the flowing waters.

The ocean also pulls me, irresistibly, like the thrust and draw of the tide. I love her wildness, her immensity, her variety.

Yesterday I sat on the shore and watched the waves break and roll in. Each one did it differently—some slowly, gradually folding at the crest; others all at once with crash and bang and bring-out-the-whole-orchestra! The sound, the height, where on the wave the water breaks, the curve, the pattern of splash, the after leap of foam—there are so many variables. The sea performs on its sand stage a ballet, with each dancer doing her own variation on the theme.

A Psalm for High Places

We declared one day as sand castle day and dedicated our energies to battling the sea, knowing all the time who would win. Walls, turrets, towers, tunnels, we erected one sandy masterpiece, getting sore knees and red noses in the process. It had all disappeared by the next morning. As we knew it would.

Holy Spirit,
living water
from God's heart,
I thirst.

Rain on my parched dreams,
tumble me in your waves,
destroy my fantasy castles,
my sandy fortresses,
and leave me clean and open.

Then refill the fountains,
and flow through my spirit,

streams of life
in a dry land.

5. Voice

I love a secret. "Come here! I wanna tell you something!" How often as a child, eyes alight, I listened as my friend cupped hands around my ear and whispered words meant only for me. The particular message mattered little. The very fact of a SECRET singled me out as someone special, someone who knew, someone to be respected.

A secret is always whispered into a waiting silence.

With people I don't know well, silence becomes uncomfortable, a container to be quickly filled with chatter. With words I seek to impress, to defend, to attack, to manipulate, until my path becomes so cluttered with verbiage I lose myself. And I lose you, too.

I hold a shell to my ear and hear secrets from the sea. I couldn't tell you in words what they mean, but I know I am wiser for having listened.

Holy Spirit,
small voice of God,
come, here, now.

Still my heart
that continues to chatter
long after my mouth
has ceased.

Cup your hands
around my spirit
and whisper secrets
that don't have names,
sing songs without words,
stroke me with a gentle knowing

and in the waiting quiet
show me the face
of God.　　⊕

What Strange Wine

An abstainer long enough
I come to you
and drink.

What strange wine, Lord,
that leaves me
in this holy stupor

this hilarious sobriety
that clears my head
unfogs my vision

and pushes me to walk
a very straight line,
that both slakes/

awakens thirst
and compels my return
to your cup

again and again.   ✽

A Psalm for High Places

Of Deity and Bones

"Does God have bones?"
David asked me that today, Lord,
and I couldn't answer him.
Well—do you?
Have bones I mean.
His question was serious, you know.
He wants to know who and how you are.
And where, too.
And if you're like us.
I don't always know.

Bones?

You did have bones once, didn't you?
Bones and muscles and fingernails
that collected dirt, feet that tired
from miles on dusty roads
and hands that bloodied
from driven nails.
You became like us, didn't you?

Thank you for reminding me.
Now I know the answer.

Tomorrow I'll tell David again
that old old story
that even a child can understand.
About a God who filled his lungs
with earth air, tasted bread,
listened to cricket song at night,
held other four-year-olds
on his lap and personally
answered their questions.
About a God who loves so much
he put on bones
and more, much more.

Tomorrow I'll tell him.   ✿

A Psalm for High Places

September 29

(The Feast of the Archangels)

Every year on September 29
they gather.
Raphael brings the drinks,
while Michael and Gabriel
raid the pantry for caviar and taco chips.
They congregate in the fireside room,
spread the food on the table,
pull out the Parcheesi board,
and take off their shoes.
Then they sing.
They start with the old songs
—Psalm 100, the Magnificat,
"Behold, I bring good tidings"
(a favorite after all these years)—
work their way through Gregorian chants
and Martin Luther to New World
Yankee Doodle, Southern gospel,
and somewhere in the process
they sing Happy Birthday to me.

With voices like wolves,
strange, far, and wholly holy,
the archangels celebrate.
"Don't be afraid," they tell me.
Planets realign.
The juice of the sun flows free. ✤

Metaphors for Transformation

I like a quick miracle—
the slap-dash comedy
of a here's-mud-in-your-eye healing,
the hilarity of the lame man's leap,
the now-you-see-it-now-you-don't vanishing act
of the leper's sores,
the amazing multiplied bread.
I love to see him pull death
from his black forever hat,
and instantly change it to a pigeon
or a sunflower.
I wish all transformations were so quick,
so silver-slick and sudden.

The deeper changes move slowly.
The Maker nudges,
and root hairs grope in the dark,
grubbing the soil
for the words that bring life.
Sap swims slowly up the trunk,
heavy, resisting the downward pull.
In a narrow path it feels its way,
inches out to the tips of the smallest twigs.
As it goes it hums a subtle song,
a dim but certain gospel.
The tree hushes in anticipation,
waits for spring.   ✣

A Psalm for High Places

(Written from the Bolivian altiplano)

Praise the Lord!
Praise him in his sanctuary,
Andean framed and cirrus vaulted.
    In the late afternoon light
    elongated shadows
    sway their gratitude
    and every bush burns.
    The high plains blaze with praise.
    Wind whistles a litany
    in minor key
    and cuts its message through my coat,
    a piercing word and true.
    Young girls head herds
    toward home, walking into the sun.

NOTES:
pinquillo, zampoña, quena—Andean wind instruments
churango—Andean stringed instrument
"Yupaychañan"—"We praise" in the Aymara language
llama, vicuña, alpaca—Andean animals of the camel family
vizcacha—small animal, similar to a rabbit
quinua—Andean grain
Tiahuanaco—ruins of an ancient Aymara civilization
Illampu, Hayna Potosí, Illimani, Mururata—peaks in the
    Andes Mountains
Chukiagu—ancient name for the city of La Paz.

The flocks skip only in metaphor
and bleat their slow songs.
Praise the Lord!

Praise him with *pinquillo, zampoña, quena.*
Twang his worth on mandolin and *churango.*
In chorus chant, *"Yupaychañan, Yupaychañan."*
Gnarled hands and creased brown faces
reflect his image,
receive his word.
Adobe and prairie grass
house his glory.
Incense of prayer
mingles with llama dung smoke,
rises, pleases him.
See! The Lord exalts the humble
and bends his ear to the poor!
Praise him!

Praise him, creatures of the heights!
Llama, vicuña, alpaca
offer proud and swift praise.
He alone fashioned the strength
of legs, the arch of neck.
They pound the earth with joy.

Condors and hawks dip
and swoop and rise again,
giving high praise,
cutting the wind to worship.
Small creatures—guinea pigs,
vizcacha, prairie snakes—
burrowing, know his secret name
and rejoice.
Praise the Lord!

Praise him, earth!
Clap before him!
Lay down your offerings!
The fields, bow low, rise, bend,
feathering the air
with their gentle harvest dance.
Wheat and barley heads sway.
Quinua purpley praises,
and underground
even potatoes know
that the Lord of the Harvest
is also Lord of the Dance.
Praise him!

A Psalm for High Places

Praise him in the yesterday rocks,
    the blue and silver stones,
    the silence of *Tiahuanaco,*
    for he was,
    and is
    and evermore will be.
    Bow quietly before him and
Praise!

Praise him in the heights!
    Bright *Illampu, Hayna Potosí,*
    Illimani, Mururata,
    white angels, guardians,
    praise him splendidly.
    "Lift up your eyes
    unto the hills,"
    is a commandment easily obeyed here.
Praise him!

Titicaca!
Praise him deeply, hilariously!
    Light skips off the white caps
    and a cold wind fills sails
    with gladness.

Be joyful quickly, for the Lord has spoken!
From his words alone poured forth these waters.
    Totora reeds bend low
    before such magnificence,
    and from deep down
    frogs give comic obeisance
    only he can hear.
Praise the Lord!

Praise him boisterously,
    cacophony of thunder,
    hail on tin roofs,
    a dark wind that howls his might.
    Fear him.
    Tremble.
    For the lightning destroys
    and the darkness screams
    the terrible names
    of God.
Worship his awful ways.
Yes! Praise the Lord!

A Psalm for High Places

Praise him in the brash and bustle
of *Chukiagu*, city of uncertain peace,
inverted ant hill,
pulsing with motion and noise.
Praise his energy,
his activity,
his ongoing creative life.
Praise the Lord!

Praise him in the cold wind
and the slanting light!
Praise him in the high thin air!
Let everything
that has breath
praise the Lord!
Yes! Praise him!
Praise the Lord!　　❀

The Cleansing

And it came to pass that Jesus, King, was passing
through the grass lands of Burundi and as he
entered a village ten leopards approached,

slinking between the huts, pad-padding down
the paths on great pudding feet,
ten shadow beasts brought low by mange and

malice came near and said to the King of Cats,
O Master, Jesus, have mercy on us,
we know if you will you can make us clean,

heal our hides, sharpen our claws, restore our
terror names, and Jesus, Beast, said,
I will, be clean, and straightway the ten

leopards were healed and with leaps and holy
yowls they departed, but one, when he saw
he was healed, returned and crouching purred

his praise, a gravelly grace song, and Jesus,
Cat, twitched his tail
while all the skies of Africa sang.   �֍

A Psalm for High Places

Credits

Thanks are due to the editors of the following magazines and books, in which some of the poems first appeared:

MAGAZINES

Christianity Today
"The Leader"

Evangelical Friend
"Of Deity and Bones," "The Spare," "A Psalm for Public Speakers," "From Bolivian Mud," "Prayer from the Plane"

Quaker Life
"Joyful Noise," "Tomato Judgment," "The Key Is Fish Lips"

Radix
"What Strange Wine"

The Other Side
"Metaphors for Transformation," "The Cleansing"

Word Process
"Metamorphosis"

World Vision Magazine
"The Image"

BOOKS

Of Deity and Bones:
A Book of Poems by Nancy Thomas
1983. Newberg, OR: The Barclay Press.
"Superior," "On Catching Frogs," "Everlasting," "Manners," "Of Deity and Bones"

Truth's Bright Embrace:
Essays and Poems in Honor of Arthur O. Roberts
P. Anderson and H. Macy, eds. 1996. Newberg, OR: George Fox University Press.
"An Ecumenical Quaker Draws the Line," "God at 'Penguins,'" "A Psalm for High Places"